Tony Hawk

Tony Hawk

Michael Bradley

BENCHMARK BOOKS

MARSHALL CAVENDISH
NEW YORK

Benchmark Books
Marshall Cavendish
99 White Plains Road
Tarrytown, NY 10591-9001
www.marshallcavendish.com

Library of Congress Cataloging-in-Publication Data

Bradley, Michael, 1962–
Tony Hawk / by Michael Bradley.
p. cm.—(Benchmark all-stars)
Includes bibliographical references and index.
ISBN 0-7614-1759-1
1. Hawk, Tony—Juvenile literature. 2. Skateboarders—United States—Biography—
Juvenile literature. I. Title. II. Series.

GV859.813.H39B72 2005
796.22'092'2—dc22

2004003523

Photo Research by Regina Flanagan

Cover Photograph by AP/Wide World Photos

V. J. Lovero/Icon Sports Media: 2–3; Tony Donaldson/Icon Sports Media: 6, 9, 10, 36, 38,
39; J. Grant Brittain: 12, 14, 18, 20, 21, 22, 27, 28, 30; Getty Images: 16; Robert Beck/Icon
Sports Media: 23, 29; Richard Mackson/Sports Illustrated: 24; AP/Wide World Photos: 34,
41; Icon Sports Media: 40; Shelly Castellano/Icon Sports Media: 42.

Series design by Becky Terhune

Printed in Italy

1 3 5 6 4 2

Contents

A wonderland for fans of extreme sports, the Boom Boom HuckJam was created by Tony Hawk.

CHAPTER ONE

The Best of the Best

To the casual observer, it was like a controlled riot. Ninety minutes of loud music and crazy stunts. What was the point? Who would want to see this?

As it turns out, plenty of people. The occasion was the first ever Tony Hawk Boom Boom HuckJam, held in Las Vegas on April 27, 2002, and it was as close to perfection as possible for fans of skateboarding, BMX bike stunts, and freestyle motocross could come. Here, under one big top, were some of the biggest names in extreme sports. Hall of famers like boarder Bob Burnquist and BMXers Dave Mirra and Mat Hoffman were all showing their stuff, while popular rock bands belted out a blistering soundtrack.

The biggest star was Hawk, who had conceived the HuckJam. "Hucking" refers to launching oneself into the air, whether on a skateboard, bike, snowboard, or other wheeled device. A "Jam" is a gathering of talent. And "Boom Boom" is just, well, boom boom.

Fifteen years ago, the thought of seven thousand people paying good money to see such a spectacle was unheard of. Skateboarding may have been popular in parks with kids sporting baggy pants and funny-looking sneakers, but it was hardly something that could excite the average American. The same went for BMX stunt riding or motocross tricksters. They were all on the fringe of the sports and entertainment world. At least until Hawk burst onto the scene. At a time when bumper stickers like "Skateboarding is not a crime" were popping up, Hawk took the whole extreme sports world into the mainstream. Not only is he the best ever to hit the half-pipe, but he has grown into a savvy businessman who understands how to tap into the huge youthful market craving wilder tricks and more dangerous stunts.

Not only is Hawk the "Michael Jordan of skateboarding," a true pioneer and multiple world champion, but he is also the world's number one extreme-sports ambassador. He has invented more than one hundred different tricks and won more than eighty-five contests. Hawk has also helped move the whole X Games generation from outlaw status to widespread acceptance. That's how he could convince seven thousand people to show up and watch his wild HuckJam.

"Tony is the first skateboarder who has given the world a face to put on the sport," said Stacy Peralta, who directed two skateboard movies and was once in charge of Hawk's skateboarding team. "He has become a part of American pop culture."

Of course, Hawk hasn't done it by himself. He has had help from ESPN, the all-sports network, which in the early 1990s realized that extreme sports were worthy of national television exposure. And there has been an ever-growing grass-roots army of skateboarders that has demanded attention and access to quality skate parks and equipment. Hawk has been an inspiration for them, even though at age thirty-five, he has retired from formal competition and is considered by some of the younger, edgier skaters to be out of touch with the sport. Hawk can relate to that, since his sport is for the young and the daring. But that doesn't stop him from boarding two hours a day, even though he and his wife,

> "Tony is the first skateboarder who has given the world a face to put on the sport. He has become a part of American pop culture."
> —Stacy Peralta

Tony Hawk in the air at the Boom Boom HuckJam.

Erin, are raising three children and Hawk runs a business empire that earns him an estimated $10 million a year. If you own a business with a product for teens, Hawk is the person you want to promote it. Not golfer Tiger Woods, basketball star Shaquille O'Neal, or tennis sensation Serena Williams. It's Hawk. He's hot.

How hot? Well, he has appeared on *The Simpsons*, a sure sign of celebrity. He has parts written for him on many other kids' shows, such as the animated *Rocket Power*. He

There he is, up in the air again at the X Games.

endorses a wide variety of products, from skateboarding equipment and clothing to toys and food. His *Tony Hawk Pro Skater* video games are among the hottest titles anywhere, with each new one (Activision has released four) more popular than the last. "Face it, the guy is totally golden right now," professional skateboarder Bucky Lasek said. "He could put his name on toilet paper and sell it to the world."

Tony Hawk's stardom has not come without a price. Along the way to becoming skateboarding royalty, he has been knocked out ten times, undergone knee surgery, and fallen too many times to count. But Hawk keeps on skating, even if he has ended his competitive career. To him, skateboarding is a way of life, not merely a sport. From the time he got his first board at age nine—a gift from his brother—Tony knew that he had found his calling. He practiced longer and more intensely than

> **"He's the guy with all the talent, creativity, and competitive drive."**
> **—Tommy Guerrero**

anyone else. That's why he landed the first-ever 900 (a two-and-a-half mid-air spin) in competition. That's why he continues to excite young boarders with his mere presence at events. That's why he has pushed a sport that was once looked down upon beyond anybody's dreams.

"He's the guy with all the talent, creativity, and competitive drive," said Tommy Guerrero, who was a pro skateboarder in the 1980s.

Not to mention the boom boom.

The young Tony Hawk skateboarding at a
Dogtown-sponsored event in Del Mar, California.

CHAPTER TWO

The Making of a Skate Punk

The official beginning of Tony's extreme-sport, live-on-the-edge skateboarding career came when he was nine years old. That was the day his older brother, Steve, gave him an old skateboard. It wasn't anything special, just a blue fiberglass banana board. Back in 1977 there wasn't any designer equipment like specialized trucks that attached heavy-duty wheels onto far-out boards. The board was basic, but it was just what Tony wanted.

Steve's generosity put Tony on wheels, but he had been living the daredevil's life for years already. Tony was born on May 12, 1968, in San Diego, California. His parents, Frank and Nancy, already had three children (Lenore, Patricia, and Steve), all of whom were much older than Tony.

Though Tony's forty-something parents hadn't planned on another child, Tony was here, and he was wild. From his earliest days, he tested his family's love and patience with frequent temper tantrums and crying binges. If something happened that Tony didn't like, he screamed and yelled. If things didn't get better, he screamed and yelled louder. He lasted just a couple of months at Christopher Robin Preschool, after rebelling constantly against nap time and a variety of other rules, though he was only three. As he grew up, Tony rarely ate

Nine-year-old Tony Hawk tackles his skateboard, which is quickly becoming his main sport.

a balanced diet. He refused the healthy parts of meals and insisted on having his dessert first. Again, if he didn't get his way, he staged a tantrum.

"Instead of the terrible twos, I was the terrible youth," Tony said. "I was a hyper, rail-thin geek on a sugar buzz. I think my mom summed it up best when she said I was 'challenging.'"

Things didn't improve as Tony got older. He was too *agitated* to participate in conventional sports. He "played" tennis by trying to hit the ball back at his opponent as hard as possible. If he lost a game of checkers, he would fly into a rage. When he was six, Nancy took him to an Olympic-size pool. Tony took one look at it and decided he must swim its entire length without a breath. That was hard enough for an adult, much less a six-year-old. "He was so frustrated when he didn't do it," Nancy said. "He was so hard on himself and expected himself to do so many things."

By the time Tony was eight, his parents knew they needed some help devising ways to keep him happy and in control. They asked the school psychologist to evaluate Tony, hoping to learn how best to handle him. It was a great move. The psychologist told the Hawks that Tony had an IQ of 144, which certified him as "gifted." He recommended placing Tony in accelerated classes, the better to take advantage of his superior brainpower. "The psychologist said he had a twelve-year-old mind in an eight-year-old body," Nancy said. "And his mind tells him to do things his body can't."

That explained Tony's hyper behavior. He had the goals and ideas of someone four years older than he was, but the abilities of an eight-year-old. When he couldn't do what he wanted, he became extremely upset. So, the Hawks put third-grade Tony into fourth-grade reading and math. That wasn't such a good idea, even though Tony loved math and, at the time, wanted to be a math teacher. He didn't feel comfortable with the step up and asked to be sent back to his third-grade classroom—with the promise of improved behavior.

Though his school situation was finally settled, Tony still needed an outlet for his high-energy personality. That leads us back to the day Steve presented him with the board. Steve was twelve years older than his little brother and was into surfing. So he no longer needed a skateboard. Besides, boarding wasn't exactly cool in 1977. Kids who skateboarded were considered odd. Why wouldn't they play conventional sports, like baseball and football? Tony had tried Little League baseball, but he quit not long after he started

No one would ever have thought that the skateboard Tony got from his brother Steve when he was nine would lead to fame and fortune.

riding his skateboard. It wasn't easy for his father, Frank, who had just been elected president of the local baseball league. "He stuck with it, even though I wasn't playing," Tony says. "I wasn't progressing anymore."

One day, a friend's mom took Tony and some other neighborhood kids to the Oasis, a nearby skatepark. Tony was home. He started going there every day, and his *perfectionist* personality drove him to practice tricks time and again. He soon became the best of the bunch.

"When he started getting good at skating, it changed his personality," Steve said. "Finally, he was doing something that he was satisfied with. He became a different guy. He was calm. He started thinking about other people and became more generous. He wasn't so worried about losing at other things."

It didn't matter if he got teased because some considered skateboarding a "loser" pursuit. Tony wasn't going to quit. He went to the Oasis every day, and he practiced longer and harder than anyone else. "We had to drag him home," Nancy said. "He would kick and scream, 'If I do this trick five hundred more times, I can get it.'"

He would get it, all right. Soon, the whole skateboarding world would know about young Tony Hawk.

Tony Hawk practices a frontside ollie as he masters the art of skateboarding.

CHAPTER THREE

Getting Good

Basketball practice would have to wait. Again. Tony was eleven years old and was at the Oasis—where else?!—practicing. The move was a frontside rock 'n' roll, and he couldn't hit it. Again and again he tried. Still nothing. Time marched on. Practice was about to start, and Tony finally gave up for the day.

"I wanted to stay at the park even longer but I had to run to practice," he said. "I was still wearing my knee pads when I got to the gym."

The idea that basketball was taking him away from the one thing he was sure about made Tony think. He was a skateboarder, not a hoopster. So, that night, he made an announcement to his father.

"I told my dad, 'I don't want to play other sports anymore. I just want to skateboard.'" What could Frank Hawk say? An attentive father, he couldn't miss how much Tony had grown to love skateboarding during the past two years. Though Frank had played basketball and football as a boy, Tony was different. So, Frank didn't fight him. Skateboarding won.

And then it lost. The old-fashioned freestyling version of the sport—practiced primarily on flat or slightly graded surfaces—was being replaced in the hearts of boarders by vert skating. Vert skating was performed on ramps and semicircular surfaces called half-pipes and required

more dangerous and technically difficult tricks. Operators of parks, including the Oasis, were scared off by the possibility of potential lawsuits by skaters who injured themselves. So, they shut down or took apart the parks to save themselves pricy insurance *premiums*. Tony was just getting serious, and his dream was in danger of dying.

"Skating was never widely accepted, and when it lost popularity in the late 1970s, all the skate parks closed down," Hawk said. "People didn't have anywhere to do it. But they just kept skating wherever they could, on both public and private property. So, there was sort of an outlaw image attached to it."

That's where Frank came in. Instead of pushing his son back into basketball, he banded with some other pro-skate parents and formed the California Amateur Skateboard League. He even enlisted Nancy as a part-time scorekeeper. By this

Tony Hawk hangs in the air!

time, Tony had attracted the attention of the Dogtown (a skateboard company) skate team and was asked to join. He gladly accepted and started to compete under the Dogtown banner. At his new home park in Del Mar, Tony was highly successful, winning many of the competitions he entered. But when he went to other parks, he struggled and

was often *intimidated* by the unfamiliar sur-
roundings. What did he expect? He was only
twelve years old!

About the only other thing that fired
Tony's imagination during his preteen and
early teen years was the violin. He enjoyed

expressing himself with music and liked to figure out the difficult patterns that were part
of violin music. But, in the end, like baseball, basketball, and even schoolwork, violin lost
out big to skateboarding. Though he enjoyed the instrument, Tony stopped his lessons.
Two decades later, when he turned thirty-three, a friend gave him a violin as a gift, and
he began taking lessons again.

In December 1981 thirteen-year-old Tony suffered another setback when Dogtown

As Tony Hawk gets older, he is able to perform ever
wilder moves!

went out of business. He now
had no team—but not for long.
He quickly hooked on with a
team sponsored by Powell and
Peralta Skateboards, a company
that had been started by skateboarding legend Stacy Peralta, a
former world champion. Peralta
had seen Tony skate and was
impressed, so he invited him to
join his team, the Bones Brigade.
It was a huge step. Tony would no
longer be skating with amateurs
or low-level professionals. He was

In 1983, Tony Hawk's father started the National Skateboard Association, which provided his son with places to skate.

with the big boys, like teammates Steve Caballero and Mike McGill. But they were not immediately impressed with the new kid. In fact, Tony was so intimidated by his new teammates that he often skated poorly during the Bones Brigade competitions.

Tony had another problem—school. Because skateboarding was anything but cool, and Tony had adopted the sport's lifestyle by bleaching his hair, wearing bangs that hung over his eyes, and sporting baggy shorts, he stood out from the other students, particularly the jocks. First at Serra High School, and later at San Dieguito High School (after his parents moved from Del Mar, California, to Cardiff), he was bullied and picked on. It didn't help either that he was short and wafer-thin, or that he loved computers. School was tough, and only skateboarding made him feel good about himself.

"It gave me a sense of self-confidence that I hadn't had before," he said. "The fact that I could think of something on my own and go out and perform it."

Upside down and holding a pole, Tony Hawk is tops in his field!

Things began to change for the better in 1983. First, Tony transferred to Torrey Pines High School, a much better place to be a skater. Even the school principal liked skating. Then, his father started the National Skateboard Organization. This was the big time. All the major skateboard companies supported it, and skaters around the country were ranked and sorted by age and ability. Although fifteen-year-old Tony wasn't thrilled that his dad was at every event in which he competed (like most teenagers, he was seeking freedom from his parents), he was happy for the solid competitive opportunities.

Later that summer, Tony was happier about something else. Though he was securing sponsorships and even had a skateboard with his own name on it, he hadn't won a professional event, even though he had been skating well. That changed in St. Petersburg, Florida, when Tony *unleashed* a routine that included many tricks other skaters couldn't complete. When it was over, he had won his first professional event.

It would be the beginning of a wild, successful ride.

Age eighteen, stunt artist Tony Hawk performs a flying kick-leap during practice.

CHAPTER FOUR

On the Brink of a Revolution

Winning that first competition gave Tony all the confidence he would need to become skateboarding's rising star. He was no longer intimidated by his teammates, competitors, or skating in other parks. By the time he was sixteen, Tony was doing *maneuvers* no one had ever seen on a skateboard.

"People were blown away by the things he was doing back then," Stacy Peralta said. "His style was so different, so creative . . . so dangerous."

Tony was still a wisp of a boy, short and thin. He couldn't pull his board up in midair, like most skaters did, so he began to trigger his vert moves with an ollie. Once airborne, Tony would launch into a series of spins and turns.

Like just about everything he did, Tony's ollie-heavy style drew criticism from more established skaters. They were holding onto the board, and he wasn't. He was different. But Tony didn't care. He practiced *fervently*, often four hours at a time, developing incredible stamina and building a *tolerance* for the bruises, sprains, and occasional breaks that came with vert skating. Before he retired, Tony would break his elbow, tear knee ligaments, crack his ribs, and sprain his wrists and ankles countless times. He also lost his

Skateboard Glossary

Skateboarding, like most sports, has a language all its own. Instead of talking about "touchdowns," "home runs," and "slam dunks," boarders refer to "ollies" and "grinding." Here's a quick look at some of the basic skateboarding lingo.

Air: Any point in a routine in which the entire skateboard has left the ground.

Frontside rock 'n' roll: A maneuver in which the skater rides to the top of a vert ramp or wall, hangs his wheels over the edge, kicks the back of the board, spins around, and drops back down.

Grind: Riding the "trucks," or parts that connect the wheels to the skateboard, against the edge of something, such as a curb, a railing, or a ramp.

Kickturn: A maneuver in which the back (tail) of the board is pushed down to the ground, enabling its rider to rotate the board on the back wheels with the front (nose) in the air.

Ollie: Invented by Alan "Ollie" Gelfand, this maneuver allows a skateboarder to get into the air by kicking the tail of the board down onto the ground and jumping up to allow the board to get off the ground.

Street skating: A form of skateboarding that involves everyday items found on or near streets, such as curbs, rails, park benches, or ledges. Skaters perform tricks on the various objects, or small ramps, found in some skateparks, rather than performing more technical maneuvers on vert ramps or bowls.

Vert: The part of any ramp that has a vertical grade and extends from ground to sky.

front teeth. He didn't care. Tony was building a great reputation among the skating community, and he wasn't about to stop. "It was just all about self-expression," he said.

Well, not entirely. As Tony neared his sixteenth birthday, he also began to make some money. Pretty good money. After a first, disastrous attempt at marketing his own skateboard through Powell and Peralta (he sold one skateboard), the company redesigned the board, replacing Tony's hawk logo with a screaming hawk skull that had an iron cross behind it. That was more like it. Kids started to buy the boards in bulk, drawn by the logo, but also by Tony's success. At the same time, Peralta filmed a video with his Bones Brigade crew. It featured them performing their whole arsenal of tricks and had plenty of footage of Tony. He was becoming popular, and his royalty checks from the company reflected it. He was only fifteen years old and already earning $3,000 a month.

> "People were blown away by the things he was doing back then. His style was so different, so creative . . . so dangerous."
> —Stacy Peralta

Tony was bulking up his reputation in competition, too. Though he was often unhappy with his performances, in large part because of his perfectionist personality, he was placing in most events and winning some. Every successful showing earned him points in the National Skateboard Association (NSA) standings. By the end of 1983, he held the most points of all NSA skaters. He was declared the best skater in the world.

He repeated the feat in 1984, even though he was still unhappy with his skating. What's worse, he was haunted by his inability to land a 540 McTwist, which teammate Mike McGill had invented. The whole skating world was energized by the new move, which featured one and a half revolutions on the board, while airborne, with a flip. Like everybody else with a board, Tony practiced day and night, hoping to land one of his own. When he finally did it—"it was the stinkiest 540 of my life," he said—Tony had proven that he had the talent and determination to pull off difficult tricks.

"Sometimes I have an idea and go to the skatepark and try it out," he said. "It may not work, or I look at the ramp and I don't even want to try it. But other times, I try something and then, wow! a new trick!"

Again, Hawk defeats gravity with a tailgrab over the hip!

Tony and his father work together to finish a new skatepark.

Tony kept trying new things. And he kept winning contests. He was voted top skater again in 1985 by the NSA. That was exciting, and it helped Tony's bank account swell. By 1985 Tony was earning $70,000 a year through prize money and royalties from equipment and video sales and deals with sponsors. When he competed, different manufacturers paid Tony to wear a helmet or a T-shirt bearing their logos. He had bought a house, even though he was still a senior at Torrey Pines High School. As one might expect, the home

Tony Hawk seems to be separated from his skateboard but remains the master of his sport.

became a haven for skaters and party central for high schoolers all over the area. Tony had gone from the bullies' favorite target to the absolute definition of cool. Part of it had to do with just growing up. By the time he was seventeen, Tony was 6' tall. And though he weighed just 135 pounds, he wasn't the runt anymore. The added height and weight gave him more strength and allowed him to try more technically difficult and dangerous tricks. Tony also benefited from the growth of skateboarding.

As the 1980s rolled on, he became more successful in competitions—and wealthier. At age nineteen, he was earning $200,000 a year. That was mind-boggling, especially considering where skateboarding was when Tony turned professional. But the good times wouldn't last. Skateboarding was in for another tough stretch, but Tony would be instrumental in helping it recover.

Hawk performs a tributary rocket air at Missle Park in San Diego, California.

CHAPTER FIVE

The Explosion

By 1993 Hawk was still considered the top skateboarder in the world—for what that was worth. The sport was suffering through another down cycle, this one created by the rivalry between vert skaters—like Hawk—and street skaters, who worked their tricks on rails, stairs, and anything else they could find. The street bunch considered themselves purer than the vert guys, because they were trying more dangerous stunts and weren't getting paid.

Though Hawk had built up a tremendous reputation and considerable bankroll through his performing and endorsements, he was still struggling in 1993. In 1990, he had married Cindy Dunbar, whom he had known since 1984. They had a son not long after getting married, so Tony had to support a family and pay a mortgage on his home in Fallbrook, California. It wasn't easy. Tony was the most recognized skateboarder in the world and had been jetting all over the planet giving demonstrations and competing. But the NSA and skateboard companies were losing money in the early 1990s, as America's youth turned their attention to other interests. At one point, Cindy was making more money as a manicurist than Tony was from boarding.

The X Games

Most of the country didn't know anything about sports like skateboarding, BMX bike riding, and motocross when ESPN launched the first Extreme Games in 1995. The all-sports network invited extreme athletes from all over the world to Rhode Island and televised their competitions.

Within a couple of years, the renamed X Games were a smash hit. Cities all over the United States tried to convince ESPN to let them host the games. Suddenly, sports like street luge (racing a wheeled "sled" down a street track) were being introduced to a whole new audience.

In 2001 the X Games came to Philadelphia, and tens of thousands of fans turned out to see them. They stayed in Philly in 2002, and even more people attended. The finals of events like BMX and vert boarding filled the city's biggest arena. Imagine twenty thousand people cheering on skaters and bikers.

The X Games gave extreme sports a giant boost and helped make them seem legitimate in the minds of many who had thought of them as fringe pursuits before. And they helped make stars out of people like boarders Tony Hawk and Bob Burnquist and BMX rider Mat Hoffman.

"I did demos [skatepark demonstrations] where I could count the spectators on two hands," Hawk said.

A 1993 survey conducted by American Sports Data Inc. revealed that there were 5.4 million skateboarders, half as many as there had been six years earlier. Hawk was able to speak to that directly. He and fellow skater Per Welinder had launched their own company—Birdhouse Industries—in 1991. That meant leaving the Bones Brigade and Stacy Peralta, who had done so much to help Hawk. That was traumatic. But the first few years at the helm of Birdhouse were even tougher. Hawk needed to invest a lot of his own funds to start Birdhouse. And since he was young, he hadn't thought ahead, so he hadn't saved much in previous years. Money was so tight that Hawk had to sell his beloved Lexus and buy a Honda Civic. Worse, he cut his daily Taco Bell allowance (Hawk was crazy about the Bell) to a mere $2.50. He took out a second mortgage on his home. And when the Birdhouse team traveled, it did so not in a jet but in a beat-up van.

By 1995 things began to pick up again. And ESPN decided to jump on the breaking wave by sponsoring the Extreme Games (later changed to the X Games) in Rhode Island.

Hawk competed and won the vert competition and placed second in the street event. It was a big moment for him. Even though he had won numerous competitions through the NSA and was known by boarders everywhere, he hadn't made any move into mainstream culture. By winning at the X Games, he had crossed over.

"Never underestimate the power of television," Hawk said. "I never liked the way they manufactured rivalries between skaters, but TV made a difference."

A big difference. Hawk's X Games performance had made him a star. When anybody spoke of skateboarding, they mentioned Hawk. Birdhouse products started to fly off shelves, as the sport began to regain its lost popularity—and then some. Tony began to get strong sponsorship deals again, and the Birdhouse team's travel conditions improved dramatically. No more sleeping in a van or crowding into a small hotel room. Hawk purchased a big RV that had a PlayStation, bar, VCR, and driver. Everybody had his or her own hotel room wherever the team stopped.

Things were going well, but Hawk was not spared personal tragedy. In the summer of 1995, his father died after a bout with cancer. Though they had argued when Tony was a teenager over how much control Frank Hawk had over his son's skating life, they had an extremely close relationship. Frank had encouraged Tony's career in ways few other parents would have. For that, Tony would always be grateful.

The late 1990s were a time of *unprecedented* growth for skateboarding and all extreme sports. Hawk was on top of the wave. Birdhouse products were selling in huge quantities. The team's exhibitions were attended by thousands, and Hawk continued to excel. At the 1997 X Games vert competition, he unleashed what was to that point the most amazing skateboard run of all time. Though he was twenty-nine years old, a virtual dinosaur in the sport, Hawk nailed four 540-degree spins in a row. He won the gold medal easily. "The combination of tricks was incredible," said Bob Burnquist, another top-notch boarder. "Tony is the man. He's my role model."

After an instructional clinic, Tony Hawk signs autographs at the Girls and Boys Club of Santa Monica, California.

The 1997 X Games were merely a warm-up. By 1998 he had won twelve world championships, earned more than $1 million in prize money and endorsement fees, and invented more than fifty tricks. It was an amazing resumé for someone in a sport that wasn't considered "major," like baseball, football, or basketball. At the 1999 X Games, Hawk cemented his status as the world's best and elevated himself to legendary status.

He had first thought about doing the 900 in 1986, but it was too hard. In 1999, at the age of thirty-one, Hawk decided it was time. He picked extreme sports' biggest stage, the X Games. With eight thousand fans cheering him on, Hawk completed the first-ever frontside 900. The trick involved two-and-a-half spins in midair—and a perfect landing. "It was my greatest personal achievement," Hawk said. Over the years, attempts to perfect the 900 had cost Hawk a broken rib and a painful spine injury. "I was either going to nail it or be carried off on a stretcher," he said.

When he landed the 900, Hawk made an announcement: He was retiring.

Sort of.

Tony Hawk flips up his board at the
Encinitas, California, skatepark.

CHAPTER SIX

One Busy Retirement

Hawk may have "retired" from competitive skating after sticking the 900 at the 1999 X Games, but the thirty-one-year-old wasn't about to start listening to oldies songs or look for comfortable rocking chairs. On the contrary, as skateboarding's biggest personality and most innovative businessman, he was faced with the challenge of remaining true to his sport's roots, while also becoming more closely associated with the corporate world.

At the same time, Hawk had become a more involved family man. He had remarried in 1995 and by 2002 was raising three boys—Riley (from his first marriage), Spencer, and Keegan. Life was getting busy, but Hawk was loving it all. To be able to make a living doing what you loved was truly the American dream.

"Here is what skateboarding is to me," he said. "It's my form of exercise, my sport, my means of expression since I was nine years old. It's what I love. I never expected it to give me anything more than that."

It had. And it continued to do so. Even though Hawk was done competing, he wasn't going to stop skating. By 2000, he and some friends had launched Tony Hawk's Gigantic Skatepark Tour, which traveled from city to city showing off the skills of some of the sport's

The legendary skateboarder hits the ramp at the 1998 X Games.

masters and stressing how much fun skateboarding was, rather than how competitive it could be. There were tricks, loud music, autographs, and plenty of giveaways from companies with whom Hawk had partnered.

One of Hawk's most successful endorsement projects was his video-game line. At first, no company wanted to go near the idea. Hawk's first meeting with Nintendo was a disaster. "As soon as I got there, the guys in the suits were like, 'Why do we want to do a skateboarding game?'" Hawk said. "They didn't get it." Soon they would, the hard way. A company called Activision contacted Hawk in late 1998 with a desire to get into sports gaming. Since others had already introduced football, basketball, and baseball products, Activision was looking for something different—like extreme sports. A year later, Tony Hawk's Pro Skater hit the stores, and it was an immediate smash. It has been so successful that Hawk earns $6 million a year from the game alone.

The video game is just part of a giant business empire Hawk had built. It's funny how a sport that seemed ready for the graveyard in the early 1990s was now rolling along. A survey by Sports Data Inc. found that more kids under eighteen skateboarded (10.6 million)

Tony Hawk in the air at the 2000 X Games.

in 2001 than played baseball (8.2 million). So, it was natural that the sport's number one personality would hit it big.

How big? In 2002, Hawk had his own collection of skateboards and equipment, a clothing line and signature shoes. He was doing commercials for food products such as Bagel Bites, had a contract with Hot Wheels to market toy cars and a remote-control skateboard, and had hooked up with Tech Deck to pitch mini skateparks and boards. The bottom line? Sales of $250 million a year and a profit of $10 million annually for Hawk.

"If you're a manufacturer, and you've got a product that you think will appeal to an audience that's under twenty-one years old, you've got to look real hard at Tony, maybe even more than some of the big names in mainstream sports," said Keith Bruce, a vice president at Foote Cone & Belding, an international advertising agency.

Hawk can now eat as much Taco Bell as he wants. And he no longer has to worry about how he'll make the mortgage payments on his house, as he once did. It's nice that skateboarding has provided him with such a good living. It's still fun, too. He has introduced Riley to the sport, and his oldest child has shown interest and talent. "The stuff he's doing

The Tony Hawk Foundation

There have always been plenty of ball fields and basketball courts available for kids in just about every city, town, or countryside village. But when it comes to places where skateboarders can hang and practice, it's a different story.

Some people are afraid of boarders. They dress differently. They don't always look like everyone else. When they hit a park or town square, some people get worried. They want them out. But there aren't a lot of spaces dedicated to boarding. That's why Hawk created the Tony Hawk Foundation. Its goal is to promote and fund the construction of parks where skateboarders can enjoy their sport without getting hassled.

Hawk began the foundation in 2001 with a $125,000 donation, which he won when he appeared on ABC TV's *Who Wants to Be a Millionaire* show. Hawk has added some of his own money and also takes a percentage of profits from Hawk Clothing for the foundation. Activision, which creates and distributes the *Tony Hawk Pro Skater* video games, gave $50,000 in late 2001.

Since its inception, the foundation has played a big role in the construction of more than sixty high-quality skateboard parks. It has worked with local officials, as well as experienced designers, to give skateboarders their own spaces. In addition, the foundation donates funds to various children's charities throughout the United States.

The crowds look on as Hawk performs another awesome feat at the X Games.

now—the basics—weren't invented until I was at least sixteen," Hawk said. "His is a whole new era. It is exciting for me to see that he's taken an interest. I encouraged him to try other sports, but this is what he has chosen."

Skateboarder Tony Hawk shows his moves at a demonstration before a game at Toronto's SkyDome.

While Hawk still skates himself, in exhibitions and just for the fun of it, street skaters and some others look down on him. "I've heard all the criticism," Hawk said. "Kids all think I'm old, and I'm a dinosaur, and I [stink]." But that's not stopping him. His Tony Hawk Foundation has donated hundreds of thousands of dollars to build more than sixty public skateboarding parks all over the country. The HuckJam doesn't roll across America looking only for money. Hawk enjoys the contact with his fans and the joy of popping onto a vert ramp for a run. Skateboarding has always been fun for Hawk, and now that it's his job, he considers himself lucky to be going to "work" with his board.

It's been a long ride since the early days, and Tony Hawk had enjoyed it all. And like skateboarding, he never knows what's coming next.

But he loves it.

stats

Stats

Tony Hawk

Born:	**May 12, 1968**
Birthplace:	**San Diego, California**
Height:	**6'2" (188 cm)**
Weight:	**170 lbs. (77 kg)**
High School:	**Torrey Pines High School**

Career Highlights

1983: Top overall point scorer in National Skateboard Association competition.

1984: Top overall point scorer in National Skateboard Association competition.

1985: Top overall point scorer in National Skateboard Association competition.

1995: Finishes first in vert competition and second in park competition at X Games.

1996: Finishes second in vert competition and seventh in park competition at X Games.

1997: Finishes first in vert doubles and vert competitions at X Games. Finishes sixth in vert-overall at World Cup Skateboarding Championships.

1998: Finishes first in vert doubles and third in vert competition at X Games. Finishes first in vert competition at World Cup Skateboarding Championships. Wins best-trick competition at Triple Crown Championships. Wins vert competition at Globe Shoes World Cup.

1999: Finishes third in vert competition and wins best-trick competition at X Games. Finishes second in street competition at B3 Championships. Wins vert competition at Glissexpo Festival.

2000: Finishes first in vert doubles competition at X Games.

2001: Wins vert doubles and finishes second in best vert-trick competition at X Games.

2002: Wins vert doubles and finishes third in best vert-trick competition at X Games.

Source: http://www.espn.com

GLOSSARY

agitated—Upset or angry.

fervently—Done with great feeling, emotion, and commitment.

intimidated—Caused to be afraid by someone or something else.

maneuver—A planned and controlled movement that requires skill.

perfectionist—Someone who is so committed to doing things completely right that anything short of that is unacceptable.

premiums—The money paid by someone for a contract of insurance on one's life, health, or possessions.

tolerance—The body's ability to withstand stress, pain, or injury.

unleash—Let loose; in this case, come up with new acts and perform them.

unprecedented—Never before seen or done.

Find Out More

Books

Boughn, Michael, and Joseph Romain. *Tony Hawk* (Champion Sports Biography). Toronto, Ontario, Canada: Warwick Publishing, 2001.

Christopher, Matt, text by Glenn Stout. *On the Halfpipe with . . . Tony Hawk.* New York: Little, Brown & Co, 2001.

Hawk, Tony, with Sean Mortimer. *Tony Hawk: Professional Skateboarder.* New York: Regan Books, 2002.

Web Sites

Sports Illustrated for Kids
http://www.sikids.com/news/video/tonyhawk/

Tony Hawk Foundation
http://www.tonyhawkfoundation.org

Tony Hawk Official Web Site
http://www. tonyhawk.com

INDEX

Page numbers in **boldface** are illustrations.